DATE DUE

GAYLORD

Today he uses sweet words and honeyed talk to those whom he entices; tomorrow he puts them to death for fabricated crimes.

Lin Liguo, son of Lin Biao, Mao's defense minister and one-time ally

For Elijah, a font of living water

Illustrations by XNR Productions, Inc.: 4, 5, 8, 9
Cover art, page 8 inset by Mark Summers
Chapter art by Raphael Montoliu

Library of Congress Cataloging-in-Publication Data
Heuston, Kimberley Burton, 1960–
Mao Zedong / Kimberley Heuston.
p. cm. — (A wicked history)
Includes bibliographical references and index.
ISBN-13: 978-0-531-20756-7 (lib. bdg.) 978-0-531-22356-7 (pbk.)
ISBN-10: 0-531-20756-0 (lib. bdg.) 0-531-22356-6 (pbk.)
1. Mao, Zedong, 1893–1976—Juvenile literature. 2. Heads of
state—China—Biography—Juvenile literature. I. Title.
DS778.M3H625 2010
951.05092—dc22
[B]

2009034157

Tod Olson, Series Editor
Marie O'Neill, Art Director
Allicette Torres, Cover Design
SimonSays Design!, Book Design and Production
Content consultant: Mark C. Elliott, Department of East Asian
Languages and Civilizations, Harvard University

© 2010 Scholastic Inc.

1 2 3 4 5 6 7 8 9 10 R 19 18 17 16 15 14 13 12 11 10   23

A WICKED HISTORY™
20TH CENTURY

Mao Zedong

KIMBERLEY HEUSTON

Franklin Watts®
An Imprint of Scholastic Inc.
New York   Toronto   London   Auckland   Sydney
Mexico City   New Delhi   Hong Kong
Danbury, Connecticut

The World of
MAO ZEDONG

Mao turned China into a communist state and ruled
it with an iron fist for almost three decades.

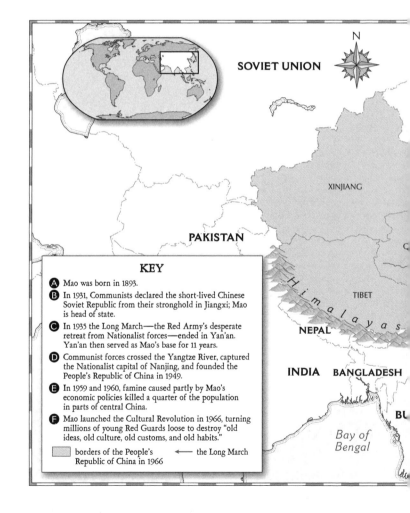

SOVIET UNION

N

XINJIANG

PAKISTAN

TIBET

NEPAL

H i m a l a y a s

INDIA   BANGLADESH

BU

Bay of
Bengal

KEY

Ⓐ Mao was born in 1893.

Ⓑ In 1931, Communists declared the short-lived Chinese
Soviet Republic from their stronghold in Jiangxi; Mao
is head of state.

Ⓒ In 1935 the Long March—the Red Army's desperate
retreat from Nationalist forces—ended in Yan'an.
Yan'an then served as Mao's base for 11 years.

Ⓓ Communist forces crossed the Yangtze River, captured
the Nationalist capital of Nanjing, and founded the
People's Republic of China in 1949.

Ⓔ In 1959 and 1960, famine caused partly by Mao's
economic policies killed a quarter of the population
in parts of central China.

Ⓕ Mao launched the Cultural Revolution in 1966, turning
millions of young Red Guards loose to destroy "old
ideas, old culture, old customs, and old habits."

borders of the People's   ⟵ the Long March
Republic of China in 1966

MANCHURIA

HEILONGJIANG

JILIN

INNER MONGOLIA

MONGOLIA

LIAONING

NORTH KOREA

JAPAN

🄵 Beijing

Tianjin

HEBEI

SOUTH KOREA

NINGXIA

🄲

GANSU

Yan'an

SHANXI

SHANDONG

Yellow Sea

NA

SHAANXI

HENAN

🄴

JIANGSU

Nanjing

🄳

Shanghai

HUBEI

Wuhan

ANHUI

Hangzhou

SICHUAN

Chongqing

HUNAN

Changsha

JIANGXI

ZHEJIANG

Pacific Ocean

🄰

🄱

Shaoshan

Jinggang Mtns.

FUJIAN

Yudu

GUIZHOU

TAIWAN

AN

Liuzhou

GUANGDONG

GUANGXI

Guangzhou

NORTH VIETNAM

HAINAN

South China Sea

PHILIPPINES

LAND

miles

0   250   500

0   250   500

kilometers

TABLE OF CONTENTS

A WICKED WEB

A look at the allies and enemies of Mao Zedong.

Family

MAO RENSHENG ———— WEN QIMEI
Mao's father   his mother

LUO YIXIU   YANG KAIHUI
Mao's first wife   his second wife

HE ZIZHEN   JIANG QING
his third wife   his fourth wife

Royalty

PU YI
last emperor of the
Qing Dynasty

MAO ZEDONG

Nationalists

SUN YAT-SEN   CHIANG KAI-SHEK
leader of Nationalist revolution   leader of Nationalists after Sun

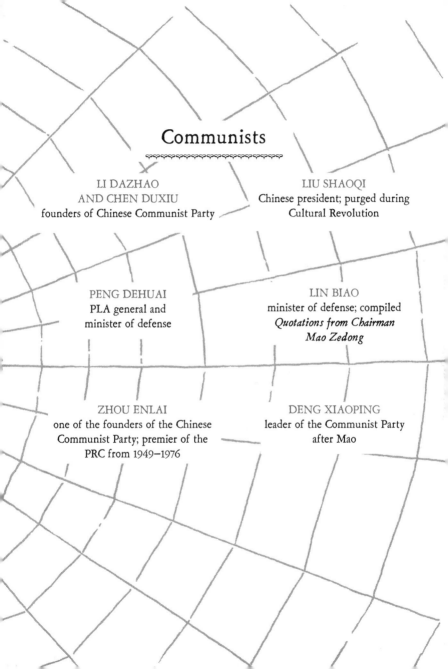

Communists

LI DAZHAO AND CHEN DUXIU
founders of Chinese Communist Party

LIU SHAOQI
Chinese president; purged during Cultural Revolution

PENG DEHUAI
PLA general and minister of defense

LIN BIAO
minister of defense; compiled *Quotations from Chairman Mao Zedong*

ZHOU ENLAI
one of the founders of the Chinese Communist Party; premier of the PRC from 1949–1976

DENG XIAOPING
leader of the Communist Party after Mao

IN THE SUMMER OF 1958, THE MOST powerful man in China claimed that the future had never looked brighter.

According to Mao Zedong, chairman of the ruling Communist Party, China would soon be the richest nation on earth. In the countryside, peasants were reporting huge increases in food production. In the cities, builders were constructing 1,000 new factories.

China, Mao promised, would go from a nation of desperately poor peasants to the world's top industrial power in just 15 years.

It was an outrageous claim—and one of Mao's top aides, Peng Dehuai, wasn't buying it. China had almost no industry to start with, and its 550 million peasants could barely grow enough food to feed themselves. How could such enormous changes happen so quickly?

THREE YOUNG CHINESE WOMEN turn an irrigation wheel with their feet at a communal farm in 1956.

Peng decided to visit his hometown in Hunan province and see for himself what was happening in the countryside. What he found left him in despair over the future of China.

In Hunan, thousands of people had been pushed to the edge of starvation. Peasants had been moved onto huge state-run farms known as communes. Mao claimed the communes produced food more efficiently than private farms. But the government took a large portion of the harvest and left the peasants with little to eat.

Many of the communes didn't even have the equipment needed to work the fields. In addition to farming, peasants had been ordered to build small furnaces to produce steel for China's new industries. Rakes, hoes, and other farm tools had been melted down into steel.

Residents of the communes, many of whom Peng knew from his childhood, lived in terrible conditions. They slept on bamboo mats with thin blankets that failed to keep them warm. They had no cooking oil and survived on a ration of vegetable leaves and a few grains of rice.

Despite their weakened condition, the peasants were expected to work till they dropped. "People are beaten up when they can't fulfill their work quota," Peng wrote, "beaten up when they are late going out to work, beaten up even for saying things [the Party workers] don't like."

Horrified, Peng gave half the money he had brought with him to the kindergarten at his local commune. The other half he gave to elderly workers. Then he sent a telegram to Mao, urging him to lower his production goals to take some pressure off the Chinese people.

Mao, however, was not inclined to listen. "Deaths have benefits," he had told Party leaders several months earlier. "They can fertilize the ground."

Mao's so-called "economic boom" was causing more deaths than anyone—except Mao himself—could imagine. In fact, it had already set in motion one of the most devastating famines in history. Before it was over, at least 25 million Chinese would die of starvation.

As tragic as it was, the famine was only part of Mao's legacy. Before Mao died, he would rob hundreds of millions of people of their homes, their history, and their humanity.

PART 1

A BLOODY MARCH TO POWER

CHAPTER 1

Boy of Stone

A young peasant boy in China
longs to ESCAPE
THE COUNTRYSIDE.

ON DECEMBER 26, 1893, A BOY WAS BORN to a Chinese farmer named Mao Rensheng and his wife, Wen Qimei. The Maos lived in Shaoshan, a remote farming community in the province of Hunan. They owned two and a half acres of rich farmland, which made them wealthier than most of their neighbors.

In the beginning the only remarkable thing about their son was his good health; his two older brothers had died in infancy. Qimei believed that her third son survived because she had taken him to a nearby rock that was said to have magical powers. She gave him the name Zedong, but nicknamed him Shi San-yazi, which means "Boy of Stone."

As Mao grew, the nickname seemed to describe him well. He was sturdy, determined, and stubborn. He adored his mother but resented his demanding father. Rensheng was an ambitious, hard-driving ex-soldier who expected his son to work as hard as he did.

When Mao was eight years old, his father reluctantly agreed to send him to school. Rensheng hoped that an education would prepare Mao to manage the family farm. But Mao preferred reading, arguing about ideas, and writing poetry. After his evening chores were finished, he read novels in bed for hours, hiding the light of his oil lamp from his father with a piece of paper.

Mao did well in school—when he wasn't picking fights with adults. His teachers found him rude and argumentative. He was expelled from at least three schools before his fourteenth birthday.

MAO POSES FOR A PHOTOGRAPH at his
parents' house in Shaoshan. The photo was taken when
Mao (far right) was about 20 years old.

Finally, his exasperated father told Mao that his
student days were over. Rensheng arranged for Mao
to marry Luo Yixiu, a young woman from a nearby
peasant family. Mao was expected to start a family with
her and settle into life as a farmer.

But the headstrong boy couldn't bear the thought of following in his father's footsteps. China was changing fast, and Mao wanted to be a part of the future. When his wife died just a year into their marriage, he left farm life for good, determined to get a modern education.

At the age of 16, the Boy of Stone was on his own.

A CRUMBLING EMPIRE

FOR THOUSANDS OF YEARS, CHINA'S EMPERORS ruled one of the most advanced civilizations on earth. The Chinese invented gunpowder, paper, and the magnetic compass. They made beautiful ceramics, jade carvings, and paintings.

Europeans coveted the luxuries produced by the great Chinese civilization. In the 1700s, Spanish, British, and Dutch traders brought shiploads of silver to China to exchange for silk, porcelain, and tea. Chinese emperors welcomed the income but grew suspicious of foreign influences. They tried to confine the foreign merchants to a single port city.

LOOKING TO THE WEST

In the 1800s, the Western world gained a technological edge over the Chinese. Europeans and Americans developed the steam engine, built modern weapons, and mass-produced textiles, shoes, and clothes.

In the mid-1800s, the Western powers returned with well-armed soldiers and forced China to open its ports to Western merchants. The merchants bought luxury goods from the Chinese—and sold them opium in return.

The Qing Dynasty, the family that ruled China, was humiliated in two wars with European countries and one with Japan. The Chinese people lost faith in their government and rebelled. Millions were killed in a series of bloody civil wars. Millions more wasted their lives as addicts in opium dens.

The Qing rulers made some efforts to create modern industry and schools. But by the time Mao left home, many young Chinese were impatient with the pace of change. They decided that there was only one way out of China's mess. They had to educate themselves in Western ways. They needed to bring modern ideas and modern technology to China.

Most importantly, China needed a modern, democratic government. To get one, the people would have to overthrow their emperor.

A CHINESE OPIUM DEN. Millions of Chinese became addicted to the opium sold by Western merchants.

A New Day

Mao joins a revolution and
watches 4,000 years of tradition
COME TO AN END.

IN 1911, MAO ARRIVED WIDE-EYED IN THE
city of Changsha, Hunan's capital. He enrolled in a
school that had a library, the first he had ever seen.
He discovered newspapers and devoured them for
information about the modern world.

In a matter of weeks, he got swept up in a
revolutionary movement that had been trying for years
to overthrow the imperial government of China.

All across China, revolutionaries had been secretly

gathering weapons and recruiting soldiers from the emperor's army. The revolutionaries took their inspiration from Sun Yat-sen, the leader of China's Nationalist Party. Sun wanted to overthrow the Qing Dynasty and replace it with a modern republic whose leaders would be elected by the people.

Mao and many of his fellow students embraced Sun's cause with a passion. They cut off their ponytails, or queues, a hairstyle that had been forced on the people by their Qing rulers. When other students refused to

do the same, Mao's gang ambushed them, scissors in hand.

A REVOLUTIONARY SOLDIER CUTS OFF a man's queue in 1912. Queues were a symbol of loyalty to the Qing emperors.

In October 1911, the revolution erupted. Rebel army regiments revolted against the Qing and took over several provinces, including Hunan. By the end of the year they controlled all of southern China.

On New Year's Day, 1912, China entered a new era. The revolutionaries formed a new government—the Republic of China—with Sun Yat-sen as its president. Six weeks later, Pu Yi, the last of China's emperors, gave up his throne.

PU YI (sitting on his father's lap) became China's emperor when he was only two years old. He had just turned six when he was overthrown.

Seeds of Revolution

Communism comes to China, and Mao finds HIS PURPOSE IN LIFE.

AFTER THE REVOLUTION, MAO DECIDED to become a teacher. He enrolled at a college in Changsha, attracted by the promise of cheap room and board. He lived on the equivalent of 25 U.S. dollars a year and spent half of it on newspapers and magazines.

While Mao studied, China fell into chaos. Sun Yat-sen and his Nationalists had been thrown out of power. The dictator Yuan Shikai took over, but he couldn't hold the country together. The central government passed from one military leader to another, and the Chinese people barely paid attention.

In China's 22 provinces, local strongmen set up their own governments and terrorized the people with their private armies. These warlords used peasants like toy soldiers in destructive wars against their neighbors.

By the time Mao graduated, he had no idea what he wanted to do. "I find it all extremely confusing," he wrote to a former professor.

Mao moved to Beijing and got a job as an assistant librarian at Beijing University. He joined a study group organized by the library director, Li Dazhao, and a professor named Chen Duxiu. There, he found an answer to his questions—in the explosive ideas of the German philosopher Karl Marx.

Society, according to Marx, was divided into classes: capitalists, industrial laborers, and peasants. Capitalists owned the businesses, factories, and land. They grew

KARL MARX argued that the poor had to overthrow the rich in order to create a truly fair society. His ideas inspired revolutionaries in Russia, China, and many other countries.

wealthy by overworking laborers and peasants and keeping the profits for themselves.

Peasants, Marx said, were likely to accept the situation no matter how unjust. But industrial laborers, he predicted, would eventually revolt. They would seize all property from the capitalists and create a new society in which workers would own businesses, factories, and land in common. All decisions would be made democratically, and the wealth would be distributed equally among the people. Marx called the new system "communism."

This, according to Li and Chen, was the system that had just been put in place in Russia, China's neighbor to the north. In 1917, workers in Russian cities had launched a revolt and overthrown their emperor. Russian Marxists—who called themselves *Bolsheviks*—took control of the rebellion and declared Russia a communist state. With the help of their Red

BOLSHEVIKS STORM THE WINTER PALACE,
headquarters of the Russian government, on October 25, 1917.
The October Revolution ultimately led to the establishment
of the Soviet Union, the world's first communist nation.

Army, the Bolsheviks were taking over factories and seizing farms from landowners. The Russian Revolution was going to give land to peasants and put workers in control of their lives—or so the Bolsheviks claimed.

With help from the Bolsheviks, Li and Chen decided to start a Communist Party in China. They recruited Mao to found a branch in Hunan. Mao returned to Changsha, where he had opened a bookstore filled with communist literature. Then he gathered his old college friends and told them it was their job to "overthrow and sweep away the old order."

During the Lunar New Year holiday in January 1921, Mao and 18 friends gathered at his bookstore. They voted to become a "communist group" dedicated to the violent overthrow of the Chinese government.

Mao had found a new sense of purpose. In the past year, both his parents had died. He had gotten a job as a school principal and married Yang Kaihui, the daughter of a former professor.

But revolution had become his one true love.

CHAPTER 4

Not a Dinner Party

Mao discovers the
POWER OF VIOLENT RAGE.

BY 1923, MAO AND HIS FELLOW COMMUNISTS
had reached a dead end. They had fewer than 1,000
members, and their chance of overthrowing the
government seemed little more than a dream.

The Communists needed help, and in 1924, they
turned to Sun Yat-sen to get it. Since being thrown out
of power, Sun had been building strength in Guangdong,
a province in the south of China. His Nationalist Party
had tens of thousands of members and plans to build a
powerful army.

The Nationalists intended to use their army to unify China by force. When the right moment arrived, they were going to march northward. Along the way, they would defeat the warlords and unite the provinces. Once they reached Beijing, they would take over the government. They called their plan the Northern Expedition.

The Nationalists and the Communists joined forces, and Mao went to work for the new alliance. His job was to train Party workers to organize peasants along the route of the expedition. Peasants there, as in the rest of China, lived under harsh conditions. Few of them owned their own land. They paid high rents to their landlords in exchange for the right to work the fields. Often they were left with little to feed their families.

Mao's organizers tried to win the support of the peasants. They promised relief from the abuses of the landlords if the Nationalists and the Communists won control of China.

On July 9, 1926, the Northern Expedition got underway. Some 75,000 Nationalist soldiers marched

CHINESE PORTERS HAUL LOADS of tea through freezing mountain passes. These men and millions of other peasants lived in grinding poverty. Mao hoped to channel their suffering into a desire for revolution.

out of Guangdong province and swept north toward Beijing. They took over Hunan in a month. By the end of the year, five more provinces had fallen.

In January 1927, Mao went to Hunan to see how the peasants had responded to the success of the Northern Expedition. There he discovered the two obsessions that would guide his life for the next four decades—the tools that would make him the ruler of the most populous nation on earth. The first was the awesome power of China's 400 million peasants. The second was terror—bloody, ruthless violence that could be used to seize power and hold onto it for good.

When Mao arrived in Hunan, he was amazed to see that the peasants had virtually taken over the province. The Nationalist Army had crushed the local warlords who supported the landowners. Their victory left the peasants free to strike back against the people who dominated their lives.

Some two million peasants had formed local associations and launched a reign of terror in Hunan. They operated under the slogan, "Anyone who has land is a tyrant." Mobs arrested landowners, forced them to wear dunce caps, and paraded them through the streets on leashes. Peasants armed themselves with long spears and stormed large farms, slaughtering pigs and confiscating grain.

Here, Mao thought, was a force powerful enough to transform an entire nation. Whoever won the allegiance of China's peasants would be able to control the country.

The Nationalists, and even some of Mao's fellow Communists, worried that the peasants had gone too far. But Mao brushed their caution aside. "A revolution is not like inviting people to dinner," he insisted. "If the peasants do not use extremely great force, they cannot possibly overthrow the deeply rooted power of the landlords." It was perfectly fine for them to execute landlords, he went on, "at least one or two in each county."

These executions may have seemed fine to Mao, but wealthy Chinese and foreign observers were horrified. To them it looked as though the success of the Northern Expedition had given the Communists free reign in China. The so-called "Bolshevik menace" appeared to be swallowing the country whole. "We were all to be murdered by our own servants," worried one American resident of China.

By the beginning of 1927, Chinese business people, foreign merchants, and Western diplomats had all come to the same conclusion: The Communists had to be stopped.

They soon found just the man to do the job.

CHAPTER 5

Going Underground

Mao retreats to the mountains TO BUILD AN ARMY.

IN 1927, THE NATIONALIST PARTY HAD A new leader, a man who was perfectly suited to take on the Communists. Sun Yat-sen had died, and his replacement was a shrewd general named Chiang Kai-shek. Chiang craved power. He mistrusted his Communist allies. And he commanded the loyalty of nearly 100,000 soldiers.

In the spring, a group of business people from the city of Shanghai approached Chiang with the equivalent of three million U.S. dollars. There was plenty more money to come, they said. All Chiang had to do was eliminate the Communists.

Chiang struck swiftly. His men swept through the Communist strongholds of Hunan, Hubei, and Jiangxi in May. The ill-equipped Communist forces were overwhelmed in a few weeks. Landlords took

DEAD COMMUNISTS LIE ON A STREET in the city of Guangzhou. They were killed when General Chiang Kai-shek decided to purge the Nationalist party of its Communist allies.

revenge on the peasants who had tormented them for the past year. By June, nearly half a million Communist supporters were dead.

Communist leaders launched a few last-ditch uprisings around the country. Then they went into hiding. All that remained of the movement were a few groups of soldiers in isolated parts of the country.

Mao commanded one of these groups. He abandoned his wife and three children in Changsha. Then he led a ragged force of a thousand soldiers, workers, and peasants to Jinggang, a forbidding mountain range on the border of Hunan and Jiangxi. There, in the remote mountain villages, he set to work building the beginnings of the army that would one day conquer China.

Following the lead of Russia's Bolsheviks, Mao called his force the Red Army. His troops raided local merchants and landlords for supplies. They seized opium fields and sold the crops. The poorest peasants, whose support Mao desperately wanted, were shielded from the looting—for now.

THIS PAINTING DEPICTS MAO (tallest figure at left) leading his troops into the Jinggang Mountains. This area became known as the "cradle of the Chinese revolution" because Mao built the first rural Communist base there.

In the mountains, Mao developed the military strategy he would use for years to come. He launched hit-and-run guerrilla raids on Nationalist forces in Hunan and Jiangxi. He summed up his strategy in a short proverb and distributed it to his troops:

> *The enemy advances, we withdraw;*
> *The enemy rests, we harass;*
> *The enemy tires, we attack;*
> *The enemy withdraws, we pursue.*

By 1928, Mao led an army of 8,000 men and controlled an area with 500,000 residents. But his growing army had sucked all they could out of the countryside. And Nationalist forces harassed them continually.

Mao and his men moved down out of the mountains into the southern part of Jiangxi. There, Mao could move freely through the countryside, recruiting peasants for his army. He was determined to turn his new base into an independent state—a miniature example of what China could become under Communist rule.

Terror in Jiangxi

Mao gives one province a
TASTE OF THINGS TO COME.

Mao's RED ARMY GAINED STRENGTH
quickly in Jiangxi. By the middle of 1930, he had 40,000
soldiers under his command. He controlled villages all
across the southern part of the province. Everywhere
Mao went, he won the loyalty of the poorest peasants by
giving them land seized from their wealthier neighbors.
He also started programs to encourage literacy and
grant women greater freedoms.

But Mao and the Communists in Jiangxi were
virtually surrounded by Chiang Kai-shek and his

A COLUMN OF NATIONALIST SOLDIERS marches on a Communist position in 1929. Chiang Kai-shek had ordered his army to encircle and destroy the Communist state Mao was building in Jiangxi province.

Nationalist army. While Mao had been in the mountains, Chiang had seized Beijing and declared himself the leader of a new Chinese republic. Chiang now commanded more than a million soldiers and kept the Red Army under constant attack. He also offered a sizable reward for Mao's head.

Under siege by the Nationalists, Mao devised a strategy that took China's Communist Party in a dangerous new direction. He launched a brutal attack on the Party itself, designed to terrorize members into remaining loyal. In February 1930, he announced that the Party was riddled with "counter-revolutionaries"—

people who opposed the Party's revolutionary goals. According to Mao, they needed to be "eliminated."

The killing began with the execution of four local Party leaders. But it didn't stop there. With Mao's approval, guards started rounding up Party members suspected of disloyalty. The suspects were held in homes and makeshift prisons. Then they were tortured until they confessed their "crimes" and named other supposed traitors.

Mao's henchmen were brutal, as revealed by an investigation conducted later by the Party. First, the guards hung suspects by their hands and whipped them. "If that had no effect, next came burning with incense or with the flame of a kerosene lamp," the investigators reported. "The worst method was to nail a person's palms to a table and then to insert bamboo splints under the fingernails."

By the end of 1931, at least 10,000 suspected counter-revolutionaries had been executed. The purge had gotten so out of hand that people could be killed for refusing to carry supplies, failing to show up for Party meetings, or talking to another suspect.

Eventually, other Party leaders criticized Mao for killing people without cause, and Mao was forced to abandon the purge. Before long, however, he would draft laws to govern future campaigns against counterrevolutionaries. Convicted workers and poor peasants could confess and start over. Capitalists, landlords, and rich peasants would be put to death.

A bloody precedent had been established. In the years to come, Mao would purge the Party whenever he felt its members needed a lesson in loyalty.

In the fall of 1931, the Communists in Jiangxi got a rest from Nationalist attacks. The Red Army stopped a Nationalist assault in September. Then the Japanese invaded the Chinese region of Manchuria, and Chiang turned his attention from Mao to his foreign enemies.

Two months later, Communist Party leaders announced the formation of the Chinese Soviet Republic in Jiangxi. Mao became its head of state.

Mao spent the next two years turning life in Jiangxi province upside down. He launched investigations in local villages, examining how every resident made a living. All farmers were classified in one of four ways—as landlords, rich peasants, middle peasants, or poor peasants. Committees appointed by Party leaders took land from landlords and rich peasants and gave it to everyone else. Merchants, landlords, rich peasants, priests, and monks were banned from voting in local elections.

To the people of Jiangxi, the classifications were a matter of life and death. Those unlucky enough to be classified as wealthy could have their homes, land, and furniture taken away.

One landowner in a village called Gong Mill could not afford to pay the tax demanded by the Party. He and his two sons were "beaten and hung up," according to the man's wife. The family handed over what they had, including all their jewelry. But the man and his two sons were executed, leaving his wife and their three small children to fend for themselves.

C H A P T E R   7

The Long March

The Communists lose nearly
everything—and MAO CLAIMS
A HEROIC VICTORY.

By 1934, THE COMMUNIST EXPERIMENT IN
Jiangxi was about to come to a violent end. After failing
to keep the Japanese out of Manchuria, Chiang Kai-shek
turned once again to attack his Communist enemies.
He was determined to destroy the Red Army once and
for all.

Chiang sent nearly one million troops to encircle
Jiangxi. The Nationalists built a defensive ring of barbed
wire, concrete bunkers, trenches, and forts around the

province. Then they waited for the Red Army to starve.

Mao and the other Party leaders knew it was time to abandon Jiangxi. They ordered their men to prepare for a secret mission.

At 5 P.M. on October 16, 1934, the Red Army's 80,000 soldiers, along with thousands of local peasants, gathered in the town of Yudu. They lifted whatever they could carry and took the first steps of a journey that history would remember as the "Long March."

This dwindling force spent the next year on a grueling march across western China, fighting off hostile armies as they fled. During this exhausting trek, Mao took over formal leadership of the Chinese Communist movement.

In battle after battle, the Red Army managed to resist annihilation by the Nationalists. Finally, Mao and the other leaders decided to go north to Shaanxi province, where another group of Communists had escaped Chiang's forces.

Mao led the remains of his army into the foothills of

the great Himalayan Mountains. The men were pelted by sleet as they marched through narrow mountain passes 14,000 feet above sea level. Temperatures dropped to freezing, and the cold bit through their thin summer clothes. "Those who sat down to rest or to relieve themselves froze to death on the spot," recalled the Party leader Dong Biwu. "All along the route we kept reaching down to pull men to their feet only to find that they were already dead."

They emerged from the mountains—and entered a huge swamp in northern Sichuan province. By this time they had nothing but raw grain to eat and almost no good drinking water. Lice tormented the marchers and disease thinned their ranks. Every morning the leaders counted their ranks to see how many men had died in the night.

In October, the remains of the Red Army finally staggered into the Communist base at Shaanxi. In about a year they had marched 5,000 miles and fought more than 200 battles. Fewer than 8,000 troops remained. The rest had deserted or died.

YOUNG CHINESE COMMUNISTS march through
Shaanxi Province, where the Red Army's Long March
ended in October 1935. Most of Mao's troops died or
deserted during this retreat from the Nationalist army.

By many standards, the Long March had been a disaster. But Mao turned it into a triumph. He welcomed an American journalist, Edgar Snow, to Shaanxi. Mao and his fellow Communist leaders told Snow about the perilous journey. Snow related the stories to the rest of the world, making Mao famous and turning the Long March into a legend. The dead were remembered as martyrs and the survivors hailed as heroes.

The Party's propagandists now portrayed Mao as a military genius who was ready to fight for the good of the Chinese people. They lashed out at Chiang for allowing Japan to take over Manchuria and gave Mao the credit for saving the Red Army. Once Mao rebuilt the army, they promised, he would accomplish what Chiang had failed to do—drive the Japanese out of China.

Mao was now 42 years old. He had lost most of his men. But he had what he really wanted. After the Long March, he was the undisputed leader of the Chinese Communist Party.

CHAPTER 8

Eye on the Prize

A Japanese invasion
forces Mao, Chiang, and
the U.S. into an
UNLIKELY ALLIANCE.

MAO AND HIS SOLDIERS MADE A NEW home in Shaanxi province, with the city of Shaanxi as their capital. They built a new Communist state, much like the one in Jiangxi. Recruiters slowly replenished the ranks of the Red Army.

But in the end, the Communists were saved as much by the actions of China's Japanese enemies as by their own efforts.

In the summer of 1937, Japan's military leaders launched a full-scale invasion of China. Troops flooded south from Manchuria, seizing Beijing, Shanghai, and Nanjing by the end of the year. After Nanjing surrendered, Japanese occupation forces burned the city and massacred countless numbers of civilians.

Under pressure from his generals and the Chinese people, Chiang reached out for help in fighting off the Japanese. He reluctantly agreed to form another alliance with the Communists.

Once again, Communists all over China could come out of hiding. Students, urban intellectuals, workers, and peasants, inspired by the patriotic fight against the Japanese, flocked to join the Party.

Under Mao's direction, the Red Army spent the next eight years fighting off the Japanese, even while it competed with the Nationalists for territory in China.

In December 1941, the Japanese launched a surprise attack on the United States naval base at Pearl Harbor, Hawaii. The U.S. responded by declaring war on Japan

FIRES BURN AFTER AN AIR RAID on the city of Chongqing.
The Japanese bombed the city more than 5,000 times and killed
23,000 civilians in an attempt to lower Chinese morale.

and entering World War II. Now Mao and Chiang had a powerful ally in their war against Japanese aggression. The U.S. would give Chiang hundreds of millions in aid to fight the Japanese in China.

But while Chiang and Mao battled the Japanese, they both kept their eyes on the ultimate prize. As soon as the Japanese were defeated, they would wage a final battle for control of China. With this goal in mind, both sides tried to avoid damaging battles with the Japanese.

The Communists made tremendous efforts to recruit peasants into the ranks of the Red Army. Mao's influence spread out from his base in Shaanxi. By 1945, he was more powerful than ever. He stood as the unchallenged leader of the Communists. He commanded an army of 900,000 soldiers. One-quarter of China's population lived in Communist-run areas.

To millions of Chinese, Mao had become a hero— and he relished the attention. He rode around in the only car in Yan'an. Party members stood for hours through his speeches, taking notes on everything he said. His portrait appeared on public buildings in Communist-controlled areas. Schools were named after him and students were taught to chant, "We are all Chairman Mao's good little children."

In August 1945, the powerful Chairman received the news he had been awaiting. The Japanese had surrendered to the U.S. and would pull all their troops out of China. The final battle for the nation's future was about to begin.

THOUGHT CONTROL

IN 1942, MAO LAUNCHED A CAMPAIGN TO make sure all Party members in Yan'an thought and acted like loyal Communists. To force them into line, he used a tactic that would become all too common in the coming years: public humiliation.

Anyone suspected of disagreeing with official policy had to submit to "self-criticism." Dissenters were forced to make long lists of their alleged failings. "You had to dig into your memory endlessly and write endlessly," recalled one accused Red Army soldier. "It was most loathsome."

Prominent suspects were put on trial and publicly denounced by their fellow Party members. One writer, Wang Shiwei, was subjected to two weeks of public abuse for suggesting that Party leaders lived in luxury while most people struggled to feed themselves.

THOUSANDS OF COMMUNISTS attend a political rally in northern China in 1944.

CHAPTER 9

Final Battle

After 27 years of civil war, China is unified under CHAIRMAN MAO.

IN THE YEAR AFTER THE JAPANESE LEFT China, the shaky alliance between the Nationalists and the Communists fell apart. Once again, the two sides plunged into a bloody civil war.

At first, the Nationalists appeared to have the upper hand. Chiang commanded three times as many soldiers as Mao. His troops were better funded, better trained, and better equipped than the Communists. They had the backing of the United States, which provided hundreds of millions of dollars in military aid.

In the spring of 1947, Chiang used his impressive army to seize the Communist capital of Yan'an. Mao and the rest of the Communist leadership abandoned their base and fled into the countryside. Chiang confidently informed his American advisers that the war would be over in a few months.

But Mao had no intention of surrendering. He was convinced that he had the Nationalists right where he wanted them. "We will give Chiang Yan'an," he said to an aide. "He will give us China."

Mao took his newly renamed People's Liberation Army (PLA) deep into the Chinese countryside. Using his trademark guerrilla tactics, he retreated to lure Chiang's forces into pursuing him. As the Nationalists followed, they strayed too far from their supplies of food and ammunition. When they grew tired and ran out of food, Mao turned and attacked in force.

In the summer of 1947, Mao's general Lin Biao launched a massive counterattack. Chiang had overextended himself. He had sent his best troops to

REFUGEES FLEE THE CITY OF NANJING
as Mao's army, the PLA, closes in. Nanjing was the capital of
General Chiang Kai-shek's Nationalist government.

occupy the cities of Manchuria, where they ended up
isolated because the Communists held the surrounding
countryside. Lin's assault shredded the Nationalists,
who lost 640,000 casualties and one million prisoners.

By the end of 1947, Chiang's army, and his
government, was falling apart. Corrupt Nationalist

officers sold rations meant for the troops. Thousands of hungry Nationalist soldiers lost the will to fight and deserted. In 1948 alone, Chiang's army lost 45 percent of its manpower, while the PLA kept growing.

That fall, Mao's generals mobilized one and a half million soldiers and two million peasant reserves. They launched a final assault on China's cities. Tianjin and Beijing fell in January. Nanjing, Hangzhou, and Shanghai followed in the spring.

Chiang's hold on China had been broken. The Nationalist leader fled to the island of Taiwan, just off China's eastern coast. With him went his air force, his

MAO'S TROOPS IN SHANGHAI, six weeks after conquering the city. They are wearing U.S. helmets seized from captured Nationalist soldiers.

AT TIANANMEN SQUARE in Beijing on
October 1, 1949, Mao declared China to be a
Communist state with himself as chairman.

navy, a few remaining regiments, and the equivalent of 300 million U.S. dollars in gold, silver, and cash.

On October 1, 1949, Mao appeared before 100,000 people in Beijing's Tiananmen Square. He stood near a two-story-high portrait of himself and proclaimed the founding of the People's Republic of China (PRC). Chants of "Long live Chairman Mao!" broke out in the crowd.

To many people, it seemed as though a ray of hope had been cast across China's future. "I was so full of joy my heart nearly burst out of my throat, and tears welled up in my eyes," recalled Mao's doctor years later. "I was so proud of China, so full of hope, so happy that the exploitation and the suffering, the aggression from foreigners would be gone forever."

Certainly there were people in the crowd that day who knew about the violent purges, the torture sessions, the confiscations, and the murders. But for the moment all the suffering had been forgotten—or explained away as a necessary step toward a better world.

Mao Zedong in Pictures
The Gathering Storm

GRINDING POVERTY
When Mao was born in 1893, millions of Chinese peasants lived in poverty.

CUTTING TIES
Many Chinese blamed the Qing Dynasty for their country's problems. Here, a revolutionary cuts off a man's queue, a symbol of loyalty to the Qing.

MAO SPEAKS
Mao argued for overthrowing the government and imposing communism, a system of government that would give workers more power.

NATIONALIST LEADER

In 1927, General Chiang Kai-shek became head of the Nationalists, the largest revolutionary group in China. With his army of 100,000 soldiers, he set out to unite the entire country with himself as head of state.

DEATH IN THE STREETS

In 1927, Chiang ordered the massacre of his former allies, the Communists, in Guangzhou (shown here) and other cities. Mao escaped the purge.

MAO'S ARMY

Mao retreated to the Jinggang Mountains. There he began recruiting peasants for the Red Army.

A LONG MARCH

THE LONG MARCH

The Red Army's grueling retreat from the Nationalists ended here, in Yan'an, in October 1935. Mao and his followers made the city their base and set out to create an ideal Communist community. Young Communists (left) were drawn to Yan'an, which seemed to promise a future in which peasants and working people would have a real say in the government.

A DISASTER

During the Long March, this man's lower legs and feet were frozen and had to be amputated. Of the approximately 80,000 soldiers who began the march, only about 8,000 survived.

JAPANESE ATTACK

Japan invaded China in 1937, and Chiang Kai-shek was not able to defeat them. Here, refugees flee after an air-raid attack on the Chinese city of Chongqing in 1938.

COMMUNISTS TAKE BEIJING

After two decades of "bitter suffering and tribulations," as Mao put it, his People's Liberation Army seized China's traditional capital in 1949.

CHAIRMAN MAO

On October 1, 1949, Mao declared the birth of the People's Republic of China. The Communist Party, he claimed, "[represents] the will of the whole nation."

MORE, FASTER, BETTER

BIG PLANS

In 1953, Mao announced the first Five-Year Plan. He coaxed peasants like these rice farmers to move from small farms to large cooperatives.

MODERN MEDICINE

Mao vowed to improve health care in China. Here, a nurse (center) disinfects visitors entering the city of Chengdu.

NEW SCHOOLS

In the People's Republic of China, thousands of schools were opened to teach peasants to read and write.

A GREAT LEAP?

In 1958, Mao set even higher goals for agriculture and industry. Here, women workers pour molten steel at a plant in Shanghai.

NO STONE UNTURNED

On communes, kids as well as adults were expected to work on public-works projects such as building sidewalks.

SPARROW WAR

During the Great Leap Forward, Mao took steps to increase agricultural output. Many of his policies failed, and about 25 million Chinese died of starvation and disease.

One disastrous policy was a plan to kill all sparrows. Mao believed that sparrows eat grain. In fact, they eat mostly insects that attack crops.

MAO'S TACTICS

CULT OF PERSONALITY
The Chinese people were taught that Mao was not just a leader—but virtually a god.

LITTLE RED BOOK
In 1964, *Quotations from Chairman Mao Zedong* was published. Soldiers were told to read it every day.

CULTURAL REVOLUTION
In 1966, Mao urged young people to expose anyone suspected of opposing the revolution—even their own parents and teachers.

CITIZEN AGAINST CITIZEN

Peasants accuse a landlord (far right) of crimes committed before the revolution. During these struggle sessions, landlords were publicly humiliated—and often condemned to death.

AIRPLANE TORTURE

The accused were sometimes forced to hold their arms behind their backs for hours.

NO DISSENT

This 1968 poster denounces former president Liu Shaoqi. Liu favored economic policies that were more moderate than Mao's. Liu was publicly disgraced and kept in confinement by the Red Guards. He died from lack of medical care in 1969, but his family was not informed for three years.

69

RED CHINA

Destroying the Old

Under cover of war, Mao begins to IMPOSE HIS WILL on China.

MAO HAD WON THE BATTLE FOR CHINA—
but the country lay in ruins, ravaged by decades of civil war. Roads, trains, and ports had been devastated by bombs. Peasants were starving, their food supplies plundered by hungry soldiers.

Mao had promised power and a better way of life to millions of workers and peasants. He needed to deliver

THE RUINS OF LIUZHOU, where 100,000 Chinese were killed
or wounded defending the city from Japan. More than 26 million
Chinese were killed in wars between 1927 and 1949.

quickly or risk widespread revolt. "We should be
capable not only of destroying the old world," he said.
"We must also be capable of building the new."

But before he could rebuild the country, war struck
again. In June 1950, Communist North Korea, which
borders China, invaded the republic of South Korea. The
United States came to the aid of its South Korean ally,
hoping to keep communism from spreading across Asia.

When U.S. troops pushed into North Korea and neared the Chinese border, Mao entered the war on North Korea's side. After seven months of bloody fighting, the two sides settled into a stalemate at the border between North and South Korea.

While the war raged in Korea, Mao tried to transform China into a communist state. He began with an attempt to "stabilize social order." The campaign targeted anyone who opposed the Party's efforts to redistribute land or reorganize workplaces. "Bandits, spies, bullies, and despots," including former Nationalists, were to be rounded up and disciplined. Mao also cracked down on business people for bribery, fraud, and tax evasion.

The Party's initial intent was to punish only the most dangerous offenders. But the Korean War created an atmosphere of patriotic zeal in which the campaign spiraled out of control. When a U.S. general threatened to drop an atomic bomb on China, the Chinese people erupted in anger. Hundreds of thousands marched in protest against the Americans. Peasants and workers

WORKERS at a textile factory pledge to increase production in support of the war effort in Korea. Mao argued that the war was no time to be "lenient" on the Chinese people. In fact, "a number of large-scale executions should be carried out."

donated their crops or wages to the war effort. People raged against the American "imperialists" for trying to destroy communism in North Korea and China.

Convinced that the revolution was in danger, Party workers, peasants, and laborers carried out Mao's orders with extreme brutality. In the first six months of the campaign, at least 700,000 people were executed. Many of the killings were held in public to terrorize the rest of the population into submission. At one public trial in Beijing, 200 prisoners were paraded before a crowd and then shot in the head.

At least 1.5 million more suspects escaped execution

only to be sentenced to *laogai*, or "reform through labor." They were sent to labor camps, where guards forced them to work in mines, fields, or timber forests. Prisoners often worked 12-hour days on a ration of cornmeal and vegetable soup. Anyone who failed to meet their work quotas had their rations cut even further.

To identify suspects and enforce punishment, Mao bypassed the secret police and the military. Instead, he used ordinary citizens to police the country. Punishments were imposed by councils of peasants or workers. "Order-Keeping Committees" in villages and factories provided the suspects. They dug through people's homes and garbage in search of letters or books that might suggest anti-Communist beliefs. They listened under windows for the sound of non-Communist songs. They encouraged friends to inform on friends, children on their parents, and workers on their bosses.

By May 1953, when the Korean War ended in stalemate, China had changed dramatically. As promised, Mao had put peasants and workers in positions of power.

PEASANTS HUMILIATE two landlords by forcing them to wear dunce caps. Many people who held positions of power in pre-Communist China were publicly shamed, imprisoned, or executed.

Committees of Party workers had replaced courts of law across the country. Ordinary citizens kept order in towns, villages, and cities.

But this transformation came at a tremendous cost. At least two million people had been killed in three years, only 400,000 of them on the battlefield. Under threat of imprisonment or execution, few people dared question the wisdom of Chairman Mao.

FAKE DEMOCRACY

IN 1954, THE PEOPLE'S REPUBLIC OF CHINA adopted its first constitution. It promised its citizens freedom of speech and the right to vote.

The constitution established a government made up of local, district, provincial, and national congresses. People could vote at the local level. Then each congress elected some members to the next level of government.

But in reality, there was nothing democratic about the PRC. It was a totalitarian state ruled by the Communist Party. Mao and his inner circle made all policy decisions. Those policies were approved without debate by the lower congresses, and then enforced by Party members.

According to the Chinese constitution, all power belonged "to the people." But eventually, the Communist Party would take control of almost all aspects of Chinese life—politics, economics, the military, and culture. And as the Communist Party gained more and more power, so did its chairman, Mao Zedong.

MAO was the absolute ruler of China.

CHAPTER 11

Creating the New

Mao tries to wrench China
INTO THE 20TH CENTURY.

WITH THE KOREAN WAR AT AN END, Mao turned his attention to China's struggling economy. The country had not advanced much since Mao's childhood. It was still a nation of dirt-poor peasants. Industry was limited to factories in a few cities on the eastern coast. Only a select few Chinese—mostly Party officials—had luxuries like cars, refrigerators, or even electricity.

Most importantly to Mao, China lagged behind other nations in military technology. The People's Liberation

Army had millions of soldiers. But China lacked the industrial power to provide its army with modern guns, ammunition, tanks, and the ultimate prize—an atomic bomb. Mao desperately wanted to turn China into a superpower that could compete with the United States and the Soviet Union. In order to do that, he needed to turn China into an industrial powerhouse.

In 1953, Mao announced his Five-Year Plan, a master plan for China's economy. He set ambitious goals for the production of iron and steel, coal, cement, and electrical power. Thousands of factories were to be built and an army of workers was mobilized to staff them.

To pay for all this industrial production, Mao turned to the people who had fought for his revolution: the peasants. He insisted that China's farmers produce rice, soybeans, vegetable oil, and pork to sell overseas. Money from the farm exports would buy machinery and military technology from the Soviet Union.

Some of Mao's fellow Party leaders pointed out that the peasants couldn't afford to produce food for export. China had 22 percent of the world's population and only seven percent of its farmland. Most peasants were struggling to feed their own families. "We cannot develop heavy industry first," complained Liu Shaoqi, Mao's second-in-command. "We must raise people's living standards first."

Mao responded with indifference. "Educate the peasants to eat less, and make their gruel thinner," he replied.

But Mao also had another plan—one that would completely transform the way hundreds of millions of peasants lived and worked. Inspired by Marx and by the Soviet Union, Mao and his fellow Party leaders prepared to start a process known as "collectivization." They would coax peasants to give up farming for themselves and join cooperatives. These large farms, Mao believed, would produce crops more efficiently than smaller private farms.

At first, peasants were urged to pool their resources on a small scale. They formed Mutual Aid Teams of several families to share work animals, tools, and labor. These teams then joined together into larger cooperatives of 20 or 30 families.

Finally, in the summer of 1955, Mao made a push to complete the transformation. Under the slogan "More, Better, Faster," entire villages formed large-

PEASANTS WEED a rice field in Yunnan province. After 1953, Mao raised taxes on peasants to pay for a massive industrialization program.

scale cooperatives overseen by the Communist Party. Most land and equipment was owned in common. All food produced on common land belonged to the government. Peasants were paid for their labor, and the Communist Party took the rest in taxes to fund Mao's industrialization plan. Many peasants got to keep small private plots to raise their own food. But they were forbidden from selling the produce on the open market. By the end of 1956, all but three percent of China's peasants had joined a cooperative.

With communism firmly in place in the countryside, Mao turned his attention to the cities. In December 1955, he announced that the government would take over all private businesses within two years. All business people—from factory owners to store owners to merchants who imported goods from overseas—would no longer run their businesses for their own profit. Instead, they would give up control to the Communist Party.

China's business people were still reeling from the campaigns to suppress "counter-revolutionaries" during the Korean War. Rather than risk imprisonment or execution, they agreed to let Party officials run their businesses.

Under the Five-Year Plan, the Communist Party extended its reach into the private details of millions of workers. The most basic method of control was the *danwei*, or work unit. Party officials assigned all citizens to a *danwei* based on the type of work they did. Workers in a steel plant, for instance, might belong to the same *danwei*.

The *danwei* was like a village within a city. It provided its members with housing, a health clinic, and perhaps a fleet of cars. (Mao's China did

STEELWORKERS in Liaoning province in 1958. Mao called for steel production to triple during the Five-Year Plan.

not allow individuals to own cars.) The *danwei* also took care of its members when they retired.

In exchange for these benefits, workers gave up a tremendous amount of freedom and privacy. *Danwei* leaders kept detailed files on the activities of their members. Anyone who wanted to change jobs, move, get married, or have children had to get permission from their *danwei* leaders. If anything suspicious appeared in a worker's file, permission could easily be denied.

After eight years of Communist rule, the Chinese economy had made great strides. Factories were humming, and agricultural production was increasing by four percent a year.

But a shroud of fear and mistrust had settled over China. As one engineer complained, "No one dares to let off steam even privately in the company of intimate friends. . . . Everyone has learned the technique of double-talk; what one says is one thing, what one thinks is another."

CHAPTER 12

100 Flowers Trampled

Mao opens the door to freedom of speech—and then SLAMS IT SHUT.

BY 1957, AS THE FIVE-YEAR PLAN DREW TO a close, Mao had brought nearly all economic activity in China under the control of the government. Communist Party officials oversaw factories and farms. They set production goals for everything from sweet potatoes to steel.

Mao had real achievements he could list to silence anyone who complained that he was moving too fast.

Industrial production had increased a staggering 19 percent a year. Prostitution and the drug trade had nearly been eliminated. Mao had reduced disease by sending doctors into the countryside to train villagers in good health practices. He had also opened hundreds of schools for illiterate peasants.

China, Mao insisted, was well on the way to becoming "the number-one country in the world."

With a new burst of confidence, Mao invited the Chinese people into an open debate over the country's direction. The Party, he insisted, needed to hear from the masses to avoid losing touch with their needs. Besides, he told his fellow Party leaders, if people had a chance to voice complaints, they would be less likely to rebel.

In February, Mao introduced his new idea before an audience of 2,000. "Let a hundred flowers bloom, a hundred schools of thoughts contend!" he declared. If people debated openly, new and valuable ideas might emerge. It would become clear over time which ideas were "fragrant flowers" and which were "poisonous weeds."

Slowly, people began to speak out—in university lectures, newspaper editorials, and workplace meetings. One professor warned that the Communist Party had become the new privileged class in China. The Chinese people no longer had landlords, business people, or Nationalist warlords to oppress them, he said. Instead they had Party officials who lived in luxury while the peasants starved.

Students took up Mao's challenge even more eagerly than their teachers. In the city of Wuhan, teenagers marched on local government offices. College students published handwritten journals arguing for freedom of

CHILDREN IN A COMMUNIST SCHOOL in 1948. During Mao's rise to power, he promised to bring education to China's poor. He made good on his promise during the Five-Year Plan, opening new schools across China.

speech and free elections. At Beijing University, they covered a wall with posters calling for democracy. One poster accused the government of using "torture and detention to gouge food out of the peasants." No one should be surprised, the author insisted, if peasants decide to "throw Chairman Mao's portrait into the toilet."

For the better part of a decade, anger had been simmering across China. In a matter of weeks, it had all boiled over.

Just as suddenly, Mao decided to put the lid back on the pot. On June 8, he announced that certain people were misusing the Hundred Flowers campaign in an attempt to "overthrow the Communist Party." It was time for the criticism to stop and the "poisonous weeds" to be identified. He told Party officials that between one and ten percent of China's intellectuals were making false accusations and should be punished.

All across China, local Party workers began rounding up people who had criticized the government. The dissenters were labeled "Rightists"—people who weren't enthusiastic enough in their support of the revolution. The Rightists were denounced in public meetings meant to humiliate them and their families. Most were then deported to "reform through labor" camps. Many officials imposed quotas: five percent of intellectuals had to be found guilty.

A young student named Lin Zhao was a typical target. She had run away from home in 1949 to join the revolution. She spent summers traveling from village to village with her university classmates, organizing campaigns to denounce landlords.

In 1957, Lin trusted Mao enough to circulate a petition demanding that he honor

LIN ZHAO was imprisoned for criticizing Mao. Unlike many prisoners, she refused to confess. She continued to criticize the government while she was in prison. She used her own blood as ink.

his promises to peasants and the rest of the country. That was the last anyone heard of her for more than ten years.

Then on May 1, 1968, her mother opened the door of the family's apartment to find an official on her doorstep. "Your daughter has been suppressed," he announced. "Pay the bullet fee." After a decade in prison, Lin had been shot. Her family was being charged a penny for the bullet.

By the end of 1957, the lesson was clear: No matter what Mao said in public, the Communist Party would not tolerate criticism. Many people suspected that the entire campaign had been a trick to lure dissenters into the open so Mao could get rid of them.

In the end, over half a million people were denounced or sent to labor camps. In Hunan, Mao noted casually, Party officials "denounced 100,000, arrested 10,000, and killed 1,000."

"The other provinces did the same," Mao went on. "So our problems were solved."

CHAPTER 13

Leap into Oblivion

Mao's plans for an economic
miracle end in TRAGEDY ON
A MASSIVE SCALE.

IN 1958, MAO ANNOUNCED A SECOND FIVE-
Year Plan. It was to be even more ambitious than the
first. In just one year, he proclaimed, China would
double its agricultural production and raise its steel
output from 5.2 million tons to 30 million tons. In 15
years, it would surpass the United States, the biggest
industrial powerhouse in the world. Mao called his plan
the Great Leap Forward.

Not only would the Chinese economy churn out steel and rice, Mao promised, it would provide the people with all the consumer goods they could possibly desire. They would live in beautiful houses. Women would wear high heels and lipstick. Every town would have its own planes, and highways would double as runways.

"If capitalism can do it," Mao demanded, "why can't we?"

DURING THE GREAT LEAP FORWARD,
delegations of workers routinely marched to government
offices to report record-breaking productivity.

The impossible burden of the Great Leap Forward fell once again on China's peasants. Cooperatives were joined into huge farms known as communes. Peasants handed over the last remaining private plots of land. They gave their kitchen utensils to the commune and ate in huge communal dining halls. Prodded by Party workers, they toiled in the fields night and day. The rules allowed everyone at least six hours of sleep every two days. Anyone who slept more was suspected of avoiding their duties. Often peasants napped in the fields, posting a lookout to watch for snooping Party workers.

Just as they were adjusting to the new workloads, peasants were ordered to build the backyard steel furnaces that Mao's defense minister, Peng Dehuai, would see on his trip to investigate the effects of the Great Leap Forward. To feed the furnaces, peasants had to sacrifice everything from pots and pans to radiators and iron fences.

Even as they struggled to meet goals for steel and farm production, countless peasants were relocated to work on massive public-works projects. One huge effort enlisted 100 million people to build irrigation systems across the country. Work crews dug thousands of canals, bridges, and dams. To speed things up, Party leaders issued a new slogan known as the "Three Simultaneouslys." Engineers were urged to "Survey, Design, and Execute Simultaneously." They were supposed to measure the site, design the project, and begin construction all at the same time.

The first reports from the Great Leap Forward were astounding. Supposedly both grain and steel production had doubled in a year. "Trails have been blazed," Mao crowed. "Many things have been realized, about which we did not even dare to dream before."

But despite Mao's boasts, the Great Leap Forward was quickly turning into a dismal failure. Most of Mao's projects were disintegrating. The backyard furnace operations were run by people who had no idea how to make steel. Almost all of the material they produced was completely unusable. Before long, Mao gave up on the effort, and thousands of furnaces were left to rust in the countryside.

The irrigation project fared no better. Pressed to do everything "simultaneously," the engineers did nothing well. An 800-mile canal was abandoned in the middle of construction. Of 500 large reservoirs dug, 200 were found to be useless. When dozens more crumbled in a storm, nearly a quarter million people drowned.

In 1959, the failure of the Great Leap led to outright disaster. A terrible drought hit the countryside. Peasants who were already worked to exhaustion did not have the resources to adjust. As grain yields dropped, Mao's response was to crack down even harder. He outlawed all unauthorized travel, making it impossible to flee ravaged areas. He ordered a new effort to keep starving peasants from "stealing" the food they had grown. In some communes, children caught taking food had their fingers chopped off.

In the midst of Mao's great plan to turn China into the world's "number-one country," millions of people began to starve. Men sold their wives for much-needed cash. In the countryside, peasants resorted to cannibalism to survive.

As the signs of the disaster became clear, Peng Dehuai returned to his hometown and discovered the extent of the suffering. He made his protest in a letter to Mao and in meetings of the Party's leadership.

Mao, however, refused to admit that anything was wrong. During the two worst years of the famine, he took seven million tons of grain from government storehouses—enough to feed millions of starving people—and sold it to other countries.

By the end of 1961, at least 25 million people had starved to death. To Mao, obsessed as he was with turning China into a world power, it did not seem to matter. "Working like this, with all these projects," he told a few powerful Party leaders, "half of China may well have to die."

CHAPTER 14

Red Guards

Mao UNLEASHES AN ARMY
OF ANGRY YOUTHS
on the rest of the country.

AS THE DEVASTATION FROM THE GREAT
Leap became apparent, Mao retreated from the failure
of his plan. He forced Peng Dehuai out of office for
opposing him. But with millions of people dying of
starvation, Mao couldn't pretend that nothing had
gone wrong.

Party leaders grew brave enough to insist that China
change its course, and Mao decided to step back for

a while. He claimed that he found his official duties "fatiguing" and resigned as China's president. But he kept his position as head of the Communist Party.

In 1962, China's new president, Liu Shaoqi, admitted publicly that the Great Leap had failed. "People do not have enough food, clothes, or other essentials," he said. "There is not only no Great Leap Forward, but a great deal of falling backward."

After all the misery caused by Mao's plan, most of its policies were simply dropped. Quotas on industrial production were reduced. Huge communes were broken up into smaller cooperatives. Kitchen utensils were given to the peasants so they could cook for themselves again.

Now almost 70 years old, Mao seemed to be distancing himself from public life. He made fewer and fewer public appearances and surrounded himself with people who told him only what he wanted to hear.

But while Mao stayed in the background, he began to plan a new campaign to crush his critics. To lay the groundwork, Mao carefully worked on his public image and raised his cult of personality to a new level.

In 1964, Mao's new defense secretary, Lin Biao, published a collection of the Chairman's personal writings. The slim volume was titled *Quotations from Chairman Mao Zedong*. It became known as the "Little Red Book." Lin gave a copy to each member of the PLA and required them to read from it every day.

Lin also used the diary of an obscure soldier to encourage the people's devotion to Mao. Lei Feng had died in a military accident but left behind a diary that Mao's propaganda chiefs rewrote and circulated widely. "I felt particularly happy this morning when I got up, because last night I had dreamed of our great leader, Chairman Mao," the diary read. It went on to proclaim Lei Feng's total loyalty to the Communist Party. "I am like a toddler, and the Party is like my mother who helps me, leads me, and teaches me to walk."

By May 1966, Mao was ready to launch a new campaign to purge his enemies and restore his position as the unquestioned leader of the Party. His allies in the Party leadership announced that enemies of the revolution had "sneaked into" the Party. These so-called "revisionists" claimed that they simply wanted to slow the pace of economic change in China. But Mao charged that they were secretly plotting to seize power and put the capitalists back in control of China. Now, he declared, was the time to get rid of the "revisionists" once and for all.

The Chinese people were urged to show their devotion to Mao by exposing "revisionists" wherever they could be found. "Chairman Mao is the red sun in our heart," the *People's Daily* reported. "Whosoever dares to oppose him shall be hunted down and obliterated." Mao's picture appeared on the front page of the newspaper every day along with quotations from the Little Red Book. Party propaganda offices churned out badges and posters of Mao by the billions. Mao's allies began handing out the Little Red Book to everyone in China.

FOR THIS PHOTO-OP, STUDENTS GATHERED to read
from Mao's Little Red Book. During the late 1960s, almost
every Chinese citizen owned a copy.

Encouraged by Mao's propaganda, young people took
up the cause with startling zeal. The sons and daughters
of Party leaders recruited their friends into activist
groups in Beijing's schools. On June 2, 1966, a group of
students posted a big sheet of paper on the outside wall
of their school. Calling themselves the "Red Guards,"
they wrote that they would stop at nothing to protect
their beloved Chairman Mao. "We will be brutal!" they

promised anyone who dared to challenge Mao. "We will strike you to the ground and trample you!"

On August 18, one million Red Guards gathered in Beijing's Tiananmen Square wearing red armbands over uniforms of military green. They were there to hear Mao give his blessing to the new movement. It was to be the Chairman's first public appearance with his army of young people.

A roar erupted from the crowd as Mao stepped to the podium. His speech had begun to deteriorate, so when the cheers and chanting died down, he motioned Lin Biao to the microphones. Lin reminded the students that they had grown up hearing heroic tales of the revolution. On this day, however, China would begin a new revolution—*their* revolution.

The students, Lin said, must stamp out "The Four Olds": old ideas, old culture, old customs, and old habits. They must root out the so-called Five Black Categories— "landlords, rich peasants, counter-revolutionaries, bad elements, and Rightists"—and eliminate them all.

The Great Proletarian Cultural Revolution had begun. Before it ended, it would turn students against their teachers and children against their parents in an explosion of violence so frightening it would leave the Chinese people shaken for decades to come.

MAO ATTENDS A RALLY in Tiananmen Square in 1966. Speaking for Mao, Lin Biao (to Mao's left) urged students to wage revolution against citizens with "old ideas."

CULT OF PERSONALITY

MAO CLAIMED HE WAS CREATING A COUNTRY in which the masses were more important than any individual. But one person in China stood head and shoulders above the rest—the Chairman himself.

The Chinese people were taught not just to respect Mao, but to worship him. Statues and portraits of Mao appeared in schools, homes, and factories all across China. Workers bowed before his image in the morning to request instructions for the workday. After their shift, they reported their accomplishments to the same portrait.

This "cult of personality" helped Mao to dominate the Communist Party for 27 years. And it encouraged ordinary people to devote themselves to him at the expense of all other loyalties. "Father and mother are dear," went the lyrics of one popular song, "but dearer still is Chairman Mao."

MAO LOOMS over the Chinese people.

CHAPTER 15

ᗡᗡᗡᗡᗡᗡᗡᗡᗡᗡᗡᗡᗡᗡᗡ

The Cultural Revolution

Mao's Red Guards
TERRORIZE THEIR ELDERS.

"DON'T BE AFRAID OF CHAOS," MAO told the young soldiers of the Cultural Revolution. "The more chaos and disorder, the better."

The Red Guards eagerly followed his instructions. Schools and universities closed down all across the country so that students could devote themselves to the new revolution. Millions of young people joined

Red Guard units in urban areas. They were given free train passes to travel the country, visit the historic sites of Chinese communism, and spread the message of the Cultural Revolution. Under orders from Mao's security chief, the police stood aside while the Red Guards tortured, looted, and killed as they saw fit.

Attacking "old ideas and old culture," squads of Red Guards destroyed centuries of cultural treasures. They smashed and burned their way through libraries, museums, and temples. They tortured thousands of artists and writers. They searched homes, hauling off antique furniture, silk dresses, volumes of poetry, musical instruments, and personal photos. Huge collections of priceless artifacts were piled up in the streets and destroyed in massive bonfires.

All across the country, young people were swept up in the violence. In Fujian province, a 16-year-old Red Guard named Ken Ling was horrified by his first experience of the frenzy. He watched while friends beat an elderly teacher with broomsticks. Every time the man passed out, his tormentors revived him with cold water. Eventually he did not get up.

"The killers were a little frightened," Ling later recalled. But he returned to school the next day to witness more of the same. "After ten days or so," he said, "I became used to it; a blood-smeared body or a shriek no longer made me feel uneasy."

The Red Guards soon expanded targets to include classmates, neighbors, and local Party workers. Anyone whose parents or grandparents had been landlords, store owners, or business people came under suspicion.

The young revolutionaries humiliated their victims by subjecting them to "struggle meetings." The largest of these public trials took place in sports arenas before jeering crowds. Red Guard activists led the accused on stage where they were forced to "do the airplane" for hours, bending over at the waist with their arms held straight back. Pinned in position, victims were punched and kicked while wild-eyed interrogators accused them of crimes against the revolution.

IN THIS INSTRUCTIONAL POSTER created during the Cultural Revolution, Red Guards use the "airplane position" on a suspected enemy of the state.

Mao made sure that his political rivals were victims of the violence. Peng Dehuai, who had criticized the Great Leap Forward, was interrogated 260 times. When his jailers could not break him, they put him in solitary confinement and instructed him to confess his crimes in writing. Peng died of cancer four years later, leaving behind an autobiography that ends with the line, "I will still lift my head and shout a hundred times: my conscience is clear!"

President Liu Shaoqi, who had overturned most of the Great Leap's policies, fell next. He pleaded with Mao to let him retire to the countryside and work as a peasant. But Mao left him to the Red Guards. The former president of China and his wife, Wang Guangmei, were beaten in the airplane position while their six-year-old daughter was forced to watch. Liu died of pneumonia in prison after guards refused to allow doctors to treat him.

By the summer of 1967, China was approaching anarchy. The Red Guards had overthrown Party leaders in several provinces. Some Red Guard units had begun looting China's military bases to arm themselves. Other units battled workers' groups for control over

MAO POSES WITH LIU SHAOQI (right). Liu had been a member of the Communist Party since 1921. He also took part in the Long March. But during the Cultural Revolution, Mao denounced him.

local governments. Even Mao had to admit that his revolution was spinning out of control.

After pushing the Cultural Revolution to violent extremes, Mao abruptly decided it had to stop. He publicly accused the Red Guards of "suspecting everyone and overthrowing everyone." In July 1968, he ordered all Red Guard units to disband.

Mao put the People's Liberation Army in charge of restoring order in China. He sent PLA soldiers into the provinces to re-open schools and disperse the Red Guards. The PLA used force when necessary to get Red Guard units to lay down their arms.

Teams of PLA officers also formed new Party committees in provinces and counties all across the country. By the time they were done, only a fraction of the old leadership remained. The army now controlled most of China's local and provincial governments.

The PLA also oversaw one of the most lasting legacies of the Cultural Revolution—a program called the "Down to the Countryside Movement." For the next decade, millions of young intellectuals—former Red Guards and their victims as well—were sent to isolated villages and forced to work alongside the peasants. Manual labor would toughen them up, Mao insisted. It also kept a generation of young people from causing any more trouble.

After two years of brutal upheaval, the Chinese people were finally able to survey the damage. An entire generation of artists, scholars, and political leaders had been executed, beaten into submission, or exiled to the countryside. Thousands of priceless statues, stone carvings, and ancient texts were damaged or lost forever. Arrests and accusations would continue until about one million people had been killed.

Mao had opened the way for the destruction of the old world. No one had the courage to suggest what should be put in its place.

CHAPTER 16

Coming Apart

MAO REACHES OUT TO THE U.S. as China falls from his grasp.

IN 1971, MAO WAS 78 YEARS OLD AND IN poor health. He had reversed so many policies and denounced so many former allies that many Chinese had begun to lose faith in their "Great Leader." Nearly a billion people could recite quotes from the Little Red Book on command. Yet few of them trusted its author.

Mao, in turn, had little faith in anyone but himself. Most of his former friends had been purged and he could not bring himself to trust the few who remained.

Relations had also deteriorated between Mao and other world leaders. Fighting broke out along the border with the Soviet Union, a nation that had once been China's most important ally. Other foreign leaders were repelled by the violence of the Cultural Revolution. Many of them broke off communication with China.

Mao desperately needed a way to restore his image, both at home and abroad. As he searched for a solution, he came to an unsettling conclusion. There was only one place left to turn: the United States.

Reaching out to the United States meant reversing 25 years of hostility. The U.S. had backed the Nationalists in their bloody struggle against Mao. As soon as Mao had won, American and Chinese troops went to war over Korea. Since then, Mao had spent two decades denouncing the Americans as "imperialists" who tried to dominate weaker nations.

But Mao had a lot to gain by opening relations with the United States. Having the powerful Americans as allies would discourage the Soviets from starting a border war with China. And a visit from the U.S. president would give Mao the prestige he so badly needed. Other world leaders, he hoped, would surely follow.

The Americans also had good reasons to put their hostility aside. President Richard Nixon, just like Mao, wanted to stop Soviet expansion around the globe. And Nixon realized that China, with a powerful military and nearly one-quarter of the world's population, could be an important ally. Besides, if Mao could be convinced to expand trade with the U.S., 830 million Chinese would provide a huge market for American goods.

With both sides open to a deal, Nixon came to Beijing in February 1972. The two leaders met for an hour in Mao's study. Nixon's secretary of state, Henry Kissinger, remembered later that Mao "dominated the room." Kissinger said he could sense Mao's "overwhelming drive to prevail."

The meeting proved to be a triumph for Mao. The United States sent an ambassador to Beijing and

IN 1972, U.S. PRESIDENT RICHARD NIXON visited China and met with Mao. It was the first time that leaders from the U.S. and the People's Republic of China had officially communicated.

removed restrictions on trade with China. Many other countries did the same. A parade of foreign leaders came to visit Mao.

The new openness brought a glimmer of change to China. The most trusted Party members gained some new freedoms. Some students were allowed to study in the U.S. and Western Europe. A handful of new books from the West were translated into Chinese.

Yet for the vast majority of the Chinese people, little had changed. They lived, as they had for decades, isolated from the outside world and cut off from their

4,000-year history. Since the Cultural Revolution, most books and movies had been banned as "poisonous weeds." The education of an entire generation had been entrusted to Mao's Little Red Book and a few other approved texts.

Living conditions hadn't improved much either—in the countryside or the cities. The terrible famine of the Great Leap Forward was a thing of the past. But most peasants still lived on meager rations doled out by their cooperatives. China's urban population had swelled by 100 million. Children, parents, and grandparents often lived crammed together in a single room.

In 1976, the Chinese found a way to speak out—if only for a moment. In January of that year, cancer took the life of one of the Party's most popular leaders, Zhou Enlai.

Mao, who had shown little respect for Zhou in recent years, tried to limit the public response to his death. Newspaper and TV coverage was kept to a minimum. Workers were asked not to hold memorial meetings.

But the Chinese people completely defied the official orders. A million people lined the streets of Beijing to express their grief at Zhou's funeral. Three months later, they began to lay wreaths in Tiananmen Square in Zhou's memory. Party leaders in the city tried to ban the memorial. But people kept coming until they had built a mound of wreaths 60 feet high.

The protest ended predictably, with several hundred arrests. But Mao had been forced to witness one final comment on his 27 years of misrule.

Mao was now 82 suffering from a disease of the nervous system. By summer's end, he was bedridden, unable to speak, and drifting in and out of consciousness. He died on September 9, 1976.

MAO DIED in 1976. His body was preserved and put on display in Tiananmen Square, Beijing.

Epilogue

Mao insisted until his dying day that he had done the right thing for China. The purges, the famine, the Cultural Revolution—they had all been necessary steps to building a communist state. And communism, he claimed, was what the people wanted.

Mao had once stated with great confidence that if capitalism ever returned to China, "our grandsons will certainly rise up in revolt" and restore the revolution he had created.

But within three years of Mao's death, China's new leaders loosened some of the control that the Communist Party had over people's lives. They broke up the communes in the countryside and gave peasants private land to farm. As a result, the income of farmers tripled. Party officials also welcomed foreign businesses to China and allowed people to start their own companies. "To get rich is glorious," proclaimed Mao's successor, Deng Xiaoping.

So far, the generation of Mao's grandchildren has welcomed the changes and pressed for more. The change in policy, accelerated after 1989, has given China one of the fastest growing economies in the world.

The Chinese government still honors Mao as the country's founding father, though the Party admits that his policies were only partly successful. That is an enormous understatement. It is true that Mao achieved remarkable things during his lifetime. He was an ordinary peasant born into a country on the verge of collapse. He united his country and ended three decades of civil war. In 27 years of leadership he turned China from a nation of farmers into a growing industrial power with an atomic bomb.

But those accomplishments came at an appalling cost. While imposing communism on China, Mao caused the deaths of millions of people and ruined the lives of millions more. His land reform efforts resulted in the repression of an entire class—the landlords and wealthy peasants of China's countryside. His economic policies helped to cause the deadliest famine of all time.

Mao also waged a constant battle to force the Chinese people into thinking the way he wanted them to think. In campaign after campaign, he lashed out against anyone he perceived to be an enemy of "the people." More than ten million ended up in labor camps. Several million more were executed or driven to suicide. Countless more were tortured and disgraced.

Mao kept a certain distance from the effects of his decisions. He rarely ordered an execution himself. But he was fully aware of the pain and suffering he caused. Half of China might have to die, he joked, in order for the Great Leap Forward to succeed. It was necessary, he claimed, in order to create a society truly built for the people and by the people. Yet that society never emerged—and "the people" suffered unimaginably.

TIMELINE OF TERROR

1893

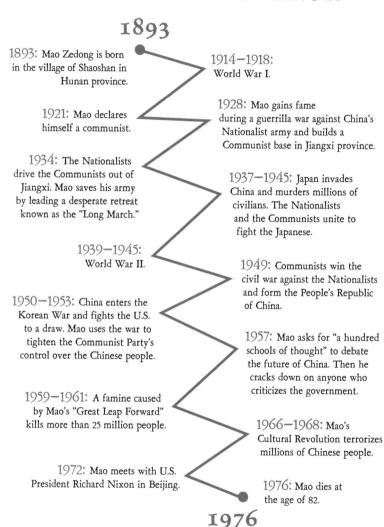

1893: Mao Zedong is born in the village of Shaoshan in Hunan province.

1914–1918: World War I.

1921: Mao declares himself a communist.

1928: Mao gains fame during a guerrilla war against China's Nationalist army and builds a Communist base in Jiangxi province.

1934: The Nationalists drive the Communists out of Jiangxi. Mao saves his army by leading a desperate retreat known as the "Long March."

1937–1945: Japan invades China and murders millions of civilians. The Nationalists and the Communists unite to fight the Japanese.

1939–1945: World War II.

1949: Communists win the civil war against the Nationalists and form the People's Republic of China.

1950–1953: China enters the Korean War and fights the U.S. to a draw. Mao uses the war to tighten the Communist Party's control over the Chinese people.

1957: Mao asks for "a hundred schools of thought" to debate the future of China. Then he cracks down on anyone who criticizes the government.

1959–1961: A famine caused by Mao's "Great Leap Forward" kills more than 25 million people.

1966–1968: Mao's Cultural Revolution terrorizes millions of Chinese people.

1972: Mao meets with U.S. President Richard Nixon in Beijing.

1976: Mao dies at the age of 82.

1976

GLOSSARY

alliance (uh-LYE-uhnss) *noun* an agreement to join forces and work together

anarchy (AN-urk-kee) *noun* a situation with no order and no one in control

annihilation (uh-nye-uh-LAY-shuhn) *noun* complete destruction

Bolsheviks (BOHL-shuh-viks) *noun* Russian Marxists who established the Communist Soviet Union after the Russian tsar was overthrown in 1917

commune (KOM-yoon) *noun* in China during the Great Leap Forward, a huge farm that was made up of smaller cooperatives; thousands of people lived together there, sharing all land, possessions, and responsibilities

communism (KOM-yuh-niz-uhm) *noun* a system in which the government owns all land and property and controls the economic and political lives of its citizens

Communist (KOM-yuh-nist) *noun* a person supporting the Communist Party of China, the Soviet Union, or another Communist country

cooperative (koh-OP-ur-uh-tiv) *noun* in China during the early 1950s, a system in which villagers joined together to share land and equipment; the food they produced was given to the cooperative, though some people were allowed to keep private plots to raise their own food

confiscation (KON-fuh-skay-shuhn) *noun* the seizure of someone's property or possessions

constitution (kon-stuh-TOO-shuhn) *noun* a document that states the system of laws in a country, the rights of the people, and the powers of the government

counter-revolutionary (KOUN-tur-rev-uh-LOO-shuhn-air-ee) *noun* a person who wanted to undo the changes brought about by a revolution

danwei (DAHN-way) *noun* during Mao's reign, a work unit to which a person was bound for life; *danwei* leaders were given strict control over the lives of their members

democratic (dem-uh-KRAT-ik) *adjective* describing a system of government in which the people hold the power, either directly or by voting to elect representatives

devastating (DEV-uh-stay-ting) *adjective* highly destructive or damaging

dissenter (di-SEN-tuhr) *noun* a person who disagrees with an idea or opinion

123

exploitation (ek-sploy-TAY-shuhn) *noun* the misuse of someone or something for selfish purposes

famine (FAM-uhn) *noun* a serious and widespread lack of food

fraud (frawd) *noun* an act of deception intended to result in personal or financial gain

guerrilla (guh-RIL-uh) *adjective* describing small groups of fighters who launch surprise attacks against an official army

humiliation (hyoo-mil-ee-AY-shuhn) *noun* deep shame or embarrassment

illiterate (il-LIT-ur-it) *adjective* not able to read or write

imperial (im-PIHR-ee-uhl) *adjective* having to do with an emperor or empire

Nationalist (NASH-uh-nuh-list) *noun* in China, a member of the political party that overthrew the Qing Dynasty with the goal of creating a modern republic; the Nationalists ruled parts of China from 1928 to 1949

opium (OH-pee-uhm) *noun* an addictive drug made from the juice of the opium poppy

propaganda (prop-uh-GAN-duh) *noun* biased information that is spread to influence the way people think

province (PROV-uhnss) *noun* a district or region of some countries

purge (PURJ) *noun* the removal or elimination of members of a group who are perceived to be disloyal

queue (KWEW) *noun* a long braid that Chinese men wore to signify their loyalty to the Qing Dynasty

quota (KWOH-tuh) *noun* a goal, set in numbers, that a person or group is ordered to achieve

ration (RASH-uhn) *noun* a fixed amount of something, such as food, that each person is given

republic (ri-PUHB-lik) *noun* a form of government in which people elect representatives to run the country

revolutionary (rev-uh-LOO-shuhn-air-ee) *noun* a person who supports the overthrow of his or her government

warlord (WOR-lord) *noun* in China in the early 1900s, a person who led his own army and had control over a particular region

FIND OUT MORE

Here are some books and websites with more information about Mao Zedong and his times.

BOOKS

Dramer, Kim. **People's Republic of China (Enchantment of the World, Second Series)**. New York: Children's Press, 2007. (144 pages) *Describes the history, geography, and culture of China.*

Gay, Kathlyn. **Mao Zedong's China**. Minneapolis: Twenty-First Century Books, 2008. (160 pages) *Particularly strong on China after 1949, this book quotes many primary sources that are available online.*

Geyer, Flora. **Mao Zedong: The Rebel Who Led a Revolution**. Washington, D.C.: National Geographic, 2007. (64 pages) *A short, well-written biography of Mao.*

Jiang, Ji Li. **Red Scarf Girl: A Memoir of the Cultural Revolution**. New York: HarperCollins, 1997. (285 pages) *The riveting true story of how a Shanghai schoolgirl and her family tried to survive the Cultural Revolution.*

Malaspina, Ann. **The Chinese Revolution and Mao Zedong in World History**. Berkeley Heights, NJ: Enslow Publishers, 2004. (128 pages) *A simply written but comprehensive book on Mao and his place in history.*

Shane, C.J., ed. **Mao Zedong: People Who Made History**. New York: Greenhaven Press, 2004. (205 pages) *A meaty collection of essays on Mao.*

Slavicek, Louise Chipley. **Mao Zedong**. Philadelphia: Chelsea House Publishers, 2004. (116 pages) *This clearly written book is particularly strong on military and political history.*

WEBSITES

http://www.pbs.org/heavenonearth/index.html
This online companion to the PBS series Heaven on Earth, the Rise and Fall of Socialism *includes a profile of Mao Zedong and an interview with scholar Merle Goldman about the evolution of Communism in China.*

http://www.pbs.org/wgbh/amex/china/index.html
The online companion to the PBS film Nixon's China Game *include historical background; profiles of Mao, Zhou Enlai, and Nixon; timelines; maps; and an interview with Henry Kissinger.*

http://www.time.com/time/time100/leaders/profile/mao.html
This informative article on Mao Zedong is part of Time *magazine's list of "100 Leaders and Revolutionaries."*

INDEX

Recently a group of Chinese businessmen approached the school at which I work. They told stories of disciplined, productive lives crowned by spectacular economic success. Their well-educated children are preparing to launch themselves into careers that will undoubtedly be as successful as their parents' were. But, they said, they cannot help feeling as though something is missing, some larger spiritual purpose.

As I listened to them speak, I thought of the Boy of Stone. Mao's dauntless determination made China wealthy and strong. At the same time, his cruel ferocity stripped many of his countrymen of their essential humanity. It was a loss that many people in China are now struggling to reclaim. My mind turned to an old Chinese proverb: "In the struggle between the stone and the water, water always wins."

Sources:

Chang, Jung and Jon Halliday. **Mao: The Unknown Story**. New York: Knopf, 2005. *This highly controversial book emphasizes personality and anecdotes rather than traditional social and political analysis.*

Kolpas, Norman. **Mao**. New York: McGraw Hill, 1981. *Although dated in places, this is a clear, comprehensive discussion.*

Short, Philip. **Mao: A Life**. New York: Henry Holt, 1999. *If you are looking for a big fat biography, this is the one to choose.*

Spence, Jonathan. **Mao Zedong: A Life**. New York: Penguin Books, 1999. *A small gem of a book by one of the world's greatest living historians.*

— Kimberley Heuston